Grey Time

Grey Time

Julia Webb

Nine
Arches
Press

Grey Time
Julia Webb

ISBN: 978-1-916760-20-2
eISBN: 978-1-916760-21-9

First published July 2025 by:

Nine Arches Press
Studio 221, Zellig
Gibb Street, Deritend
Birmingham
B9 4AU
United Kingdom

www.ninearchespress.com

Printed in the United Kingdom on recycled paper by:
Imprint Digital

Nine Arches Press is supported using public funding by Arts Council England.

Supported using public funding by
**ARTS COUNCIL
ENGLAND**

i.m Dawn Carol (1945-2010) Neil Webb (1972-2009) Dominic Campbell (1963-1987) Julian (1972-1976)

Contents

"I'll speak a bit of you to anyone who'll listen."
— **Joanna Guthrie**

"Ever since she died
she can't stop dying. She makes me
her elegy."
— **Norman McCaig**

"Believing that holes can be filled with language is
dangerous—only space itself occupies empty spaces."
— **Kristin Prevallet**

I have spent years falling out of each window

the tall building of grief gave me.
Every day I climb to the top of the tower
and let myself fall again.

Even though I have tried to stop,
feeling the guilt of the living
the groove it runs in is too well worn.

Each night as I climb
the stairs of my grief,
I pause for breath at the midway point.

Each night I hope to meet the ghost
of a loved one coming back the other way.
But there's only me and my breath.

I wonder what my dead would tell me
if I gave them voice—
perhaps, *burn the building down?*

The Hare

He brings something with him –
a chill that creeps inside the bones
and through the blood.

Winter with all its ice and snow is coming –
I feel it in the air,
hear it in the wind that shivers through the trees.

The hare feels it too.
This hare, that might be a dream or might be real
and is as big as the one I thought was my mother

in the woodland burial ground last summer,
that day when the weather was warm as a kiss
and the foliage densely lush and green,

and the map I had printed out so vague
that I couldn't find her grave.
But there they were – the hare and the deer –

crossing our path by the badger sett
and just as sudden gone again.
The hare – the biggest I have ever seen;

the same colour as that suit, hung in the gallery,
no buttons or markings – just brown felt.
I wore it in my dreams for weeks after,

my skin naked and itchy beneath its pelt.
A penance perhaps –
for not trying hard enough to find her.

Like that day in the church
when I opened my mouth to speak
and no words came.

A Geography of The Dead

(i)

underground
under root
under badger, fox, hare

under a canopy of green
we lay you there
we pray you there / here

your name is like perfume

51.18562 NORTH
-1.68479 WEST

the coordinates
we steer ourselves by

(ii)

under the flush pink of morning
under herringbone cloud
under sleet and rain and snow and hail

under searing sunlight
on this planet that
turns and turns and turns

How beautiful you are, my darling!

170 miles from the body of your son

2 hours 53 minutes by car
from your grave to his

(iii)

the boy who forgot how to laugh
the boy who ruined his liver with pills

> a 55-hour walk from where you lie
> to the place where we laid him

> *the beams of our house are cedars*
> *our rafters are firs*

we laid him down and covered him up
to the background roar of traffic

> 52.40959 NORTH
> 0.73813 WEST

the sun doing its best
to shed a little warmth
on the inhumation

on the great wide emptiness of us

> *I will search for the one my heart loves*

(iv)

and how will you reach him now mother

A303, M3, M25, M11, A11

by air or underground
by water or through the ether

I looked for him but did not find him

how will you reach any of us

Grey Time

after Rosemarie Waldrop

"Will you stop leaving now?"
– Lavinia Greenlaw

The first time

White floor, walls, waffle blanket on the bed. White
sheets, white tubular bedframe, white lid on the water
jug – though there is no possibility of any water passing
between your lips.

I remember nothing of the journey

Nothing even of the summoning phone call, though there must have been one. There's just this room, the bulk of you stilled and quieted. The white coat asks me to sign a DNR, proffers a pen. The black words crawl across the white sheet of paper. Everything so black and white in the doctor's mind – their incomprehension at my refusal to sign. My breath on your face as I try to entice you back to the world.

The hotel bedroom looks out over a carpark

and the back of a nightclub, where bouncers congregate to smoke. The sheets are white and crisp, tucked in so tight it's hard to make a space for our bodies. The window is grimy with evil-looking spikes on the outside sill. Foxy puts down his phone and tries to prise the window open a crack because I cannot breathe. The stuttering air conditioning turns the room icebox. A refrigerated lorry hums beneath our window. We watch it unload its cargo of carcasses.

*The restaurant we choose is an all-you-can-eat
Chinese buffet*

full of Saturday revellers. We feel shabby, underdressed.
We take thick china plates from the stack as instructed
and queue to fill them from numerous dishes arranged
under a giant heat lamp. The food is brightly coloured.

The puddings feel apt – white globules of peeled
lychees in a sticky glug of syrup and mint green mochi
dusted with icing sugar. Everyone else is ramping up
for a night at the clubs.

Back on the ward the white is yellowy, piss-stained

The woman in the bed opposite yours is calling for a nurse. She has a drink but needs help to drink it. You sleep on oblivious. When you finally open your eyes, their whites are pinkish. You squeeze my hand so hard the skin whitens. I send Foxy to the shop and he returns with phone and TV cards, a bottle of barley water, a packet of pens and a book of stiff white paper. Before we leave, I conquer the expanse between beds and lift the lukewarm beaker of tea off the nightstand of the woman opposite. She sucks greedily on the plastic straw. Her fingers, claw-like, grip my arm.

I think we might have taken the train home and come back again

but I can't be sure, and there is no one left to ask. You returned to yourself slowly. When you started making demands for this or that, I cried with relief.

The phone receiver crackles with static

It's as if you are calling from underwater. You have a wheelchair, you say, and enjoy whizzing along the wide white corridors of the convalescent hospital making a nuisance of yourself. I suspect the staff love you. What lies I tell myself to avoid another visit – lack of money, lack of time, work or school commitments. I wish for a miracle, wish they could hold on to you forever, but it's only temporary. In a few months the place will be closed.

The next time I see you you're at home

Your white hair puffed softly around your skull.
The hospital bed fills your tiny bedroom. You shout
instructions through to the living room – can we find a
certain book or a bottle of flower remedy? Can I bring
you a mug of instant cappuccino? I scrub the fridge and
stove top until they are pristine. Foxy vacuums a tangle
of your hair from the carpet. When the carer comes,
we're banished into the rain for an hour. We take refuge
in the gloomy church. The white cassocks of the choir
line one wall of the vestry, hanging like limp bodies on
their metal hooks.

This hospital is older, greyer

I find myself in the hospital chapel. My last time alone with you and you're solid, cold, immovable. You have nothing to say. The fabric that covers your body is white and filmy with an embroidered gold cross that I know you'd love. I wish I could stay here with you in the candlelit gloom, but I whisper my sorries and goodbyes and step back out into the glare of the day, the hostility of your friends.

For I will consider my mother

after Christopher Smart

who was a candle that illuminated with the strength of a floodlight
who was the stained-glass gift to the meanest window
who was never the stew but was always the dumpling
who filled herself with helium and floated along the ceiling
who invited in a forest, then a river, then a mountain
who hooted like an owl and cooed like a pigeon
who was born in a storm with a rainbow inside her
who stained the world purple and covered it with glitter
who some days was a guitar and other days a mouth organ
who built a snowman right there in her bedroom
who taught herself to fly but was a terrible swimmer
who had visited the stars and learnt how to shimmer
who was in love with the moon but kept the sun inside her
and when it was time for her to shine oh boy did she

She Died

and we were on the train
me with my grief
and you with your leather man-bag
your *patience of a saint*
and the train was crowded
and I was crying
and we weren't at a table
though we usually get a table
but we had booked last minute
and no one needed to face my pain
and there was horrible tea that scalded
and nowhere to put the teabag
and there might have been a sandwich
and she was still dead
and though I knew I couldn't have prevented it
part of me believed I could have
if I had just got there sooner
if I had taken an earlier more expensive train
and not believed the nurse who told me
she's fine for now come in the morning
and you put on your headphones
and buried your head in your newspaper
impatient with my grief but trying not to show it
because at that point you hadn't lost
any loved ones yourself

Wolf on My Back

I would rather have been anywhere else
than in that building at that counter
filling in the forms to get the wolf-certificate.
It was unseasonably warm,
and we had to be somewhere at a certain time
perhaps the undertakers.
I knew that town well from happier visits,
which charity shop was more fruitful.
My memory has turned the day to fur
though I know it was the beginning of spring.
Just a week later your funeral brought the sleet,
my nephew underdressed for the weather
until someone lent him a pelt,
and you nowhere in sight
though they told us you were in the casket.
I like to imagine the hunter
was staking us out from behind the stand of trees
but finding us wanting
as we surely were.

Funeral Party

I barely remember now
the shape and colour of her coffin
though I know I must have picked it out.
How solid she was for one so empty of herself –
six men it took to carry her from cart to grave
while appropriate sleet stung our hands and faces.
She should have been there carrying her staff,
her dress hem dragging in the mud,
her black hat keeping the weather from her hair
as we stood beneath dripping trees.
As they lowered the coffin, she might have sung a song
or recited a poem, in the voice I barely remember.

It was mother's ghost, hearing rain, who came to speak of sorrow

after Janice Lee

I thought I was swimming
but I was drifting further and further out

until the shore was in the distance
and the distance kept on growing

my arms and legs were heavy
and there were no lifeguards

and even if there had been
I was too far out for them to see

and I couldn't shout
losing you had ripped the words from my throat

I remembered you as a life raft
but maybe I have embellished

maybe you were something smaller
a life ring in neon orange

you were definitely bright
so bright it sometimes hurt my eyes

and now there was nothing but distance
me uselessly treading water

getting further and further from the shore

owl birth

where else could i have come from   but owl darkness
swooping down   between the pines
my mother once said
that she wasn't   in love with me
that she looked me in the eye   and said
            there you are
like i was simply   revisiting
and how was i to know
starved thing   beak endlessly open
that i was not her first
        that another had been before me
night daughter   first born
who wrenched   my mother's heart   open
and sealed it shut   with her departure
mother of the night wood
forest mother   feather mother
i thought her   mine alone back then
as i crouched   night after night
in the dark of the nest   waiting
            for her return
how weightless i was   in her presence
how alive i became   beneath her gaze
she birthed me in the cold winter
not egg borne   but owl wombed
half woman   half owl she was
half mother   half wild thing
half softness   half claw

Lecture

We perceive two objects –
the daughter and the mother.

The mother was born in April 1944,
but she was not a monster
until she was monstered by her father.

Number one daughter was born in March
the year England finally won the World Cup.
These Boots are Made for Walking at the top of the charts.

Number one daughter later found she was not number one.
You will have to attend tomorrow's lecture
if you want to hear more about that.

The daughter was monstered by the grandfather
but she has no memory of it.
The account of it was gifted to her by her mother.

The distance between daughter and mother
has moved beyond physical space and into time.

The mother believes in ghosts
but finds she is unable to haunt the daughter.

The daughter does not believe in ghosts
but wishes she did.

The mother's departure cracked something open.

The daughter remains beached on the shores of her grief.

She called her Melanie

was obsessed with Melanie.
When she saw a Melanie, or heard of a Melanie
she thought it might be her, Melanie.

Our headmaster's daughter was called Melanie,
mousy hair and fox-coloured eyes like mine.
Adopted, the mothers whispered behind their hands.

My mother was convinced that *his* Melanie
was *her* Melanie. She stalked her from afar.
But, of course, her Melanie,

was no longer called Melanie;
had been claimed by her new parents
for their own with a change of name.

But she had called her Melanie,
so always thought of her as Melanie.
It was Melanie that she remembered

soft and wriggly in her teenage arms.
She still called her Melanie
but she never found *her* Melanie

though she tried, and tried, and tried…

A small girl cries on a blue and black tiled kitchen floor

snow falls softly all around her
then in big fat flakes
her breath gasps clouds into the shivery air

her flowery Christmas dress
has stiffened in the cold
her soft pink skin turns purply blue

her legs are half buried already
but she doesn't move
just sits there as her white socks

and best red sandals are completely covered
the room is filling up with snow
it blizzards over everything

the wind whistles
through the ceiling washing lines
it wobbles her mother in her chair

snow on snow until the kitchen is full
until the girl and her mother
have completely disappeared

Julian

The boy we didn't grieve enough
according to our mother:
The neighbours' children
had to have the day off school.

Never mind that I had crept
to the top of the stairs,
the way I always did
for a late-night knock at the door.

This time it wasn't one of the Wilson kids
looking for their mother,
but Steve from the end house –
my favourite person in the world.

Their son Julian was four –
the same age as our brother.
Julian is dead he said,
his voice a hiccup, *meningitis.*

I didn't love Julian
the way I loved his parents,
but I crept back to bed
and cried myself to sleep.

Our mother's accusatory voice
was sharp and stabby.
So I offered up my truth
as shield and confession.

Impossible, she said,
I came up five minutes later
and you were fast asleep.

The same mother

who taught you to be a house
and not a tree
retaining treeness for herself
the same mother who invited
your ex-boyfriend round for tea and chat
the week after he broke your heart
so that you came home from school
and found him at the kitchen table
and *yes* he was a bit older
but not by much –
closer to your age than hers
your first real love
that same mother
didn't *steal* exactly – more *borrowed*
and each time you found him there
her roots spread deeper
into your foundations

everything

She gave me Devil's Food Cake & Victoria Sponge. She gave me burger Saturdays. She gave me a golden egg cracked into a bowl of margarine and sugar. She gave me *Lord of the Rings* & *The Hobbit* in her best voice in a dark kitchen. She gave me chicken & mushroom pie & crisps & a thwack on the head with a mop. She gave me laughter & humiliation. She gave me words slippery as seaweed & sharp as lemon juice. She gave me an outside chance. She gave me a race I could never win. She gave me tears & arguments & a second-hand bed under a draughty window. She gave me a bad feeling about myself I can't shake off. She gave me grocery shopping & dusting & polishing. She gave me curses & blessings. She gave me a locked toilet door & the inability to open up. She gave me lentil bake & curry. She gave me an overload of sweetness. She gave me reasonable doubt. She gave me a crash landing. She gave me a pain in my chest & indigestion. She gave me love but I couldn't take it. She gave me tears & accusations. She gave me herself as an adult child. She gave me everything & nothing. She gave me my life & I took it.

My father was in love with his office

Each morning, he took the sandwich he had made the night before and he walked to his office. He opened the office door and he sat in his chair. Where did he put his sandwich in the office? Where was the kettle? Where did he keep his cup of tea? My father was a very important office. He drew things on the computer. My father knew how to draw important things and how to engage in office-to-office conversation. He was more office than the office itself. When my father slept, did he dream of the office, of sitting at his desk making important decisions? Did he dream about talking on the office phone, of swivelling round on his chair? When my father was no longer the office, he was a lost thing, a crashed computer. The office had kept him upright all those years and now he was slumped and broken. There should be a special office for men like my father who have lost their office. I would like to put the office back inside my father, but I don't know how.

St John's Way

so big it's not just one street
but made up of many
as if the planning department
tired of arguing about names
decided fuck it
this half of the estate is St John's
and this half St Martin's
and this bit here by the shops
is where we'll divide it

thinking that the poor
are in need of dividing
and though we know
that dividing lines are arbitrary
we keep to our own side
and while we might pass
through St Martin's
on our way somewhere
we know St John's is our home
and mostly we stay there

Trying to Make Sense of Things

If you could hold onto anything it would be the rivers of your past
that are almost gone – Ben jumping off the high bridge to scare you,

the way your blood bloomed like a rose
when you stood on a piece of glass,

tadpoles in a bucket of the wrong kind of water,
your mother's *I told you so's* ringing in your ears.

Your mother would have let anyone take you anywhere
just so she could have a bit of peace and quiet.

Your mouth was full of fur cones, conkers, wooden chess pieces.
Matchbox cars were whizzing round inside your blood.

If you hadn't been an orange, you would have been a lemon.
If you hadn't been a pine cone, you would have been an acorn.

You wonder why you don't remember the telling
of when your great grandma died.

Were you in the dark shed with the garden tools,
your heart broken into little pieces?

Were you waiting by the letterbox
for a postcard from her that would never come.

Your great grandma was the only person in your life back then
who loved you unconditionally.

Perhaps you are still there in the dark.
Perhaps you are still in the hall waiting.

And maybe I became orange

Maybe the colour my parents painted
my childhood bedroom crept inside me
and overtook the pale powdery roses
they painted over and stained me
orange. Bright orange, like the sun
in a child's drawing, or an orange
on a photo of a tree in a distant
orchard – a place, back then, I could
only imagine. The orchard we lived in
was made of houses and its fruit were children.
My friend Samantha was beige –
these days we might call it oatmeal –
and Deborah was brilliant white, the way
the sun suddenly dazzles your eyes
when it slides out from a behind a cloud.
Only I was orange. Fizzing orange,
like a boiled sweet or a living room fire,
or the kind of football only bought
for boys back then. I liked it, or I thought
I liked it, but ever since I left home
I've been trying to tone it down.

Even if you're not

Leave home / smell rats
inhabit sewers / read books
feel dangerous / even if you're not
ride mopeds / bicycles / go too fast
have accidents / spend weeks in plaster
hitch-hike cross country / camp in fields
wake up surrounded by bullocks / hear their breath / smell it
leave home / take drugs / eat rats
feel dangerous / even if you're not
fill notebooks with your thoughts / write bad letters
light fires / set off fireworks in the house
leave home / smell dogs / fall in love with rats
play house / pretend you're something you're not
make collages / smoke roll-ups / read books
look death in the eye / try and outstare it
wear black / but not for funerals / lie awake in the dark
feel dangerous / even if you're not

A woman's hair is trailing through the mud

the river is flowing past her head
the moon shines placidly above

a light drizzle begins to fall
the evening is as black as soot or coal

her head is pillowed on the grass
her face already wet so that at first

she doesn't notice the drizzle fall
her dress is ripped and a button has come off

the river is quiet
but flows insistently past

she wonders where ducks go at night
she wonders if she should try and stand up

the grass is soft and wet beneath her head
water keeps falling from the sky

it pools at the corners of her eyes
but she doesn't move

the rain is cool and gentle
it doesn't hurt at all

the person she thought was her friend has gone
there's just the rain

the river   the grass   the mud

Commune

The house contained a hurricane
and a fire that burned the roof off.
It had a temper that came barrelling out
at unexpected moments, and once
threw a chair through a window.
Its rooms were always dark, needing
to be lit even on the brightest days.
Every corner of every room housed
a spider as big as your fist.
It was a house that welcomed bad news
and the grief that came with it.

The Messengers

The sun was trying to get into the house
blue at the windows
blue at the open door

cool flagstones on bare feet
as I worked up a sweat on the bread dough
the open mouth of the oven

as I slipped the loaves inside
the cat asleep on the Aga lid
the kind of quiet

a busy house rarely delivers
the sun trying to push its way inside
birdsong coming through the open window

the table sticky with other people's crumbs
Woman's Hour chatting away in the corner
the bread forming its crust in the oven

blue at all the windows
a deeper blue in the open doorway
two pairs of feet in black shoes

two pairs of legs in black trousers
blocking out the light
the sun shining on regardless

two uniforms with silver buttons
blue at the windows
bird song barging its way inside

Woman's Hour almost over
the bread turning black in the oven
the sun reaching in through the open door

The Magic Ritual

The night before your death
the sky was luminescent,
the sound of the sea hypnotic.

As the magician threw crystals into the fire
the flames shot up towards the sky –
blue, green, yellow, purple.

The golden couple he called us
as we headed back to the car park,
as if we were something to be envied.

And he would keep on visiting
me for months after
as if I was a tragic heroine,

when really, I had been crushed
in the car with you that morning
and left for dead at the side of the road.

Mourned

you might have
thought
 freedom   was
what you gave me
liberation   and in
a way it was
but not chosen   not
freely taken   your
leaving was the way
a cup empties itself   when
you're not looking   or
 when something
 precious drops down
between the floorboards
 or that time as a kid
when the fifty pence piece
 slipped   through the hole in
 my skirt pocket   and rolled
 along the road and into
the mouth of the drain
 nothing I could do to stop it
 it's that same feeling   in
 the pit of the stomach   like
 a flowerbed dug over and the
 treasure stolen   or an
early morning raid   by the
 drugs squad   all
               your
                  belongings
                     strewn
                        across
                           the floor

If ever there's a time for crying

I was the cold face of the moon in a sky full of glitter.

I was a shut book, my pages stuck together.

I was the driest-eyed person in the place.

My eyes burned – small suns inside dry sockets.

I was a tree standing resolute against the force of the wind.

Everyone else was showing how much they loved you.

But I was hollow at my middle.

You were oblivious under a blanket of flowers.

I was full of the emptiness you had given me.

I was a rocky island with no safe landing place.

I was the blank paper on the table at the end of an exam.

I was on top of the pyre waiting for a whiff of petrol.

His absence is like the sky, spread over everything

after C.S. Lewis

As if it has become the hare
speeding away across the twilit field
or boxing its shadow as the sun
is snared by a stand of scrubby pines

or perhaps it is jugged in the pot
the stringy muscle and sinew
stewed to a soup with onions,
red wine, juniper berries

or hung in the cool dark larder
by its hind legs, blood accumulating
in the chest cavity the way unshed tears
coagulate behind the eyes

and it hangs there and hangs there
waiting to be cut into pieces
waiting to become less
than the sum of its parts

Mourning is a young horse

careening wildly about the house
it crashes into the furniture
knocking plates and cutlery to the floor
tramples over them

the way your loss trampled
me underfoot back then
all those secrets you kept revealed
the other women who loved you

the horse of my grief
was too much for me to handle
it galloped off in any direction
no thoughts of traffic

it was trying to outrun itself
with me trailing behind it
hanging onto its reins for dear life
my hair filling with twigs and leaves

Essay on Craft

after Ocean Vuong

Because a woman woke up
and her head had become a flower.

Because the images were placed
in a way that pleased the eye.

Because if she's not careful
the scalpel can cut.

Because once a woman is glued down
it's difficult for her to become unstuck.

Because when a woman steps off the page
a prince might see an opening.

This is about violence

This is about the surprise you felt
as you lay on the kitchen floor
at your friend's house.

This is about the way
you thought you were strong
and the way that you thought

you were better than that,
but you were grieving
and you wanted to feel loved,

and his eyes saw right inside you
(or so you thought)
and sometimes a good thing

can turn into a bad thing,
and sometimes the warnings
aren't there at all.

This is about violence –
how sometimes we just don't recognise it
until it's locked inside the room with us.

I opened the door and let violence in

I cooked violence dinner

I poured violence a glass of wine

I introduced violence to my friends

I took violence to the pub

I laughed at violence's jokes

I let violence seduce me

I ran violence a bath and we got in it together

I let violence pin me down

I let violence lock me up

I showed violence I was sorry (but I was not sorry)

I slept in violence's arms

I let violence hand me the blame

I believed violence's truths (until I didn't)

If only you didn't have to shove your living in my face,

after Emma Jeremy

you said,
if only your living could be smaller, quieter,
almost like you weren't there at all.
I curled myself up into a ball.
I moved further and further into the corner
until I almost was the corner,
but you could still hear me breathing
and when the sun moved across the window
I made a shadow. My shadow, you said,
was an afront to your senses.
Look at it, you said, *grotesque thing,*
taking up so much space.
But even a shrinking violet
can't lose their shadow,
even a wallflower still needs air to breathe,
so I went on living, taking up too much space,
trying hard not to be noticed.
When we parted ways, I didn't try and follow,
I let you go and breathed a sigh of relief,
then I breathed another and another.
I sucked in as much air as I could.

You are trying to remember how you got into this mess

but your brain is full of ants
and there are windchimes
dinging away in your nerve ends
you try and shut them out
but they are persistent
you wish you weren't so intolerant
you wish you were more like your mum
who loved such frivolities
you remember the tinkling chimes
that hung in all her doorways
how they would brush against your head
as you passed beneath them
letting her know exactly where you were
at any given moment

New

The dizziness comes hourly.
I stand in the bathroom in front of the mirror.
I am an empty sack
without you inside me anymore.
They say I'm a mother, *Mum*, they call me.
Can Mum hold baby like this?
Can Mum put baby on the scales?
Baby, they call you, like you're a thing they own,
not mine at all. Not mine, though my whole being
all my waking (and sleeping) hours
are dedicated to keeping you alive.
The landlady comes to empty the meter
(or so she says) and leans into your basket,
breathes her nasty cigarette breath
into your tiny squidged up face.
New Mother they call me,
as if I'm the one who's new.

to him who came from my body

I gave the otter of me
I gave myself over
to the tending and the feeding
I was a soft spring lawn for him
and in summer when the hot sun parched it
I conjured a sprinkler from the depths of myself
and brought it back to life
I cut out the everyday from the dreams
and magic of the universe
I offered him the sun the moon
the stars the planets
all the animals of land and sea
he took what he wanted
the others he discarded
I fed him on the meat of me
bite-sized morsels
choir I was and story teller
I was the strainer
through which he poured the tea of himself
I caught those leaves and saved them
now of course he craves his own world
and I must lay down my sword and shield

son as the city he was born in

each morning after his shower
he slips his arms through streets
he can never remember the names of
he wears his city like an old jumper
one that's grown with him
he threads his way easily
through its maze of streets
but if you ask him for directions
he looks flummoxed
his body is felted with parks and car parks
his hands are cars and his feet are buses
his head is a boating pond next to a fish pond
with a headdress of heron
his voice is the sirens that haunt the night
his veins flow with shoppers and tourists
his mind is the castle on the hill
bits of it are closed for maintenance
promising something bigger and better
when the renovations are finished
something flashy and shiny
with a higher entrance fee

always more bird than woman

I made my child a nest of twigs
but he snagged himself on its thorns
said I was *a bad mother*

I never knew how to do things right
no one ever taught me
so I took myself to college

to try and learn the ways of child
but I was always pecking at the bars
of any cage I found myself in

each winter when the gales came
I took a battering
so that by spring I was tired and bedraggled

no energy left to lay another egg
and anyway I told myself
I need to try and get this one right

sometimes at the height of summer
he and I would climb up to the rooftop
and hurl ourselves off

swimming on the warm updrafts
until we were delirious
and scoured clean by the wind

I find my dead lover by
the side of the motorway

He has become an oak tree
though he doesn't seem to know it.
I have looked everywhere for you,
I say, *what are you doing here?*

I like a reminder, he says,
and, yes, I know it's perverse.
The unrelenting noise and whizz
of traffic is making my head spin.

He waves his branches
and I see that someone, a child perhaps,
has hung up pictures of fruits and vegetables –
little scraps of paper cut from magazines.

*Well at least they're keeping you
well nourished,* I say,
but he doesn't answer.

When you tell me how you feel

I know I may never fully understand it
I hear its song and feel its presence
and as with the sea
I let the talk wash over me like a tide
or the wind that waves the tops of the trees
and watch the houses passing
or I look at the road
which is not a satisfactory answer
but might be better than the nothing I offer—
not even *mm hmm*
unable to say anything at all
I sit frozen
I have already set myself up for failure
by having the thought
that I won't know how to reciprocate
thinking something is expected of me
sometimes I turn to stone
when people tell me how they feel
in certain situations
and because it's hard to know exactly how I feel
I don't put you at ease by telling you how *I* feel

I don't put you at ease by telling you how *I* feel
because it's hard to know exactly how I feel
in certain situations
when people tell me how *they* feel
sometimes I turn to stone
thinking something is expected of me
and I won't know how to reciprocate
and by having that thought
I have already set myself up for failure
so I sit frozen
unable to say anything at all
not even *mm hmm*
which might be better than the nothing I offer
but is not a satisfactory answer
or I look at the road
and watch the houses passing
or the wind that waves the tops of the trees
and I let the talk wash over me like a tide
and as with the sea
I hear its song and feel its presence
but know I may never fully understand it

You rearrange your face

into what you think she is expecting
you yearn for something
though you would be hard pushed to name exactly what
messages dance around inside their little boxes
you can't tell if they're barbed or friendly
and there is a shout inside you that sometimes rises up
you have to keep stuffing it back down
it's like swallowing a cheesy sock
you do the things that you think are expected
and then you worry that they were wrong
you try and behave politely and kindly
but sometimes a thing comes bursting out
it's like there's a Jack-in-the box inside you
you read somewhere that if you just keep smiling
that everything will turn out right

Hot House

Why do you think your mum was attracted to all those strange people? my aunt asked. We were in the hot house at Kew Gardens, the smell was wet and tropical. Tiny synchronised sprinklers were doing their watery dance. The air was full of water. I had been here, I knew, as a small child with my mother. I couldn't quite remember it but there was something familiar about the heat and the smell. I remembered the parade of 'weirdos' that had come through our house – artists, stoners, folk musicians. I remembered how we had walked all those miles to the airbase and back with placards on a hot summer's day – the day the bad thing happened to my brother in the men's loos at the park. We moved into the dry heat of the desert house with all those swollen succulents and cacti with their poisonous spines. This was the greenhouse I liked least, though there were plants that looked like tiny stones, small and perfectly formed. My aunt and I moved silently towards the exit. I don't think she knew she had overstepped the mark, but she saw that I had gone inside myself, to that same place bad news always sends me. *Is it time for the café?* she asked.

After my brother died, I let my garden get overgrown

we sat on the lawn
the guinea pigs in their little run

my son poking dandelion leaves
through the wire

my friend concerned that my boyfriend
had opted out of the funeral

well he only met him once, I told her
not seeing it for the red flag that it was

we never did tame those guinea pigs
so they remained nervous

cramming themselves into their wooden box
whenever we opened the door to their hutch

over the years that followed
the garden grew a beard of brambles

until that oblong of grass no longer existed
and the guinea pigs eventually died

I often go back to that moment in summer
the guilty tears I shed for my brother

the sunlight dancing across my son's face
as he hunted for the lushest, greenest leaves

This coffee-cup stain on this scrap of paper could be his

but did he drink coffee
so much we don't know about the brother
(his daily habits)
we know he drank beer
(or was it whisky)
but what did he eat in the morning
where did he shop
what did he put between his slices of bread
what books did he read
(if any)
did he miss his (our) mother
was he lonely
(of course he was lonely)
did he sometimes forget to take his pills
(or choose to)
did he stay inside
(or go out daily)
did he wonder how things had come to this
(like we do)
was there any way back
was it preventable
(unthinkable)
did he drink coffee or tea
or neither
(like our sister)
did he know it was coming
is there any way to ease the guilt

I wish something violet would happen

This week has been mostly red
and a little bit orange.

The forecast for next week is yellow
with a tinge of green.

I sit greyly in the garden
wishing something violet would happen.

No matter how golden the day is
my skin stays grey.

My best friend is a very purplish purple –
she rolls up her sleeves when she visits

so I can admire her purple arms.
I pretend to like them

but secretly I would prefer them paler,
a touch more grey.

My son is silver –
the offspring of greys almost always

shine brighter than their parents.

If

if I wanted
to leave
unturned
I would've found
astounded confounded
left no stone
my powers would
if I wanted to
been unbounded
corners rounded
opened cupboards
drawers boxes
if anywhere was a place
I once frequented
a let's pretend
if you were a place
if dark corners
if you wanted
if you hadn't
but there was a leaving
a headstone
if I wasn't
I would have sought
I would have fought
if I could've

without

"How would my mother find us again with so much starlight?"
  — Rachel Eliza Griffiths

I am building you an owl
claw to wingtip
hoot to wingswish
this variance
this everything
everything I can't keep right
everything I can't keep fixed
nonsensical poem this
built from words
waiting for your breath
to knock it down
owl blink
owl hush
under the trees I wait
for the suddenness of owls
and I wish you here for real
wish you back from the dead
wish you acres of owl flight
on soft summer evenings
all the smells of the woods
all the reds and golds of autumn
to dark your way back home

Notes

"I'll speak a bit of you to anyone who'll listen." 'Bobbing Along' by Joanna Guthrie, from *Her Whereabouts* (Pindrop Press, 2023).

"Ever since she died / she can't stop dying. She makes me / her elegy." 'Memorial' from *The Many Days: Selected Poems of Norman MacCaig* (Polygon, 2011).

"Believing that holes can be filled with language is dangerous—only space itself occupies empty spaces." Kristin Prevallet, from *I, Afterlife: Essay in Mourning Time* (Essay Press, 2007).

The Hare: *Felt Suit* 1970 is a two-piece suit comprising a jacket and a pair of trousers made from coarse grey felt. It is number seventy-seven in an edition of one hundred identical suits, all produced in the same year by the German artist Joseph Beuys (Tate).

A Geography of The Dead: quotes in italics are from the Bible's 'Song of Songs'. The numbers are grid references of the places my mother and brother are buried.

Grey Time: this sequence was inspired by 'White is a Colour' by Rosemarie Waldrop.

The quote is from 'My father leaving' by Lavinia Greenlaw, from *The Built Moment* (Faber and Faber, 2019).

DNR means Do Not Resuscitate.

For I will consider my mother: inspired by 'Jubilate Agno' by Christopher Smart.

Funeral Party: is a centena – a poem of exactly 100 words (excluding the title) that starts and ends with the same three words.

It was mother's ghost, hearing rain, who came to speak of sorrow: title is a line from *The Sky Isn't Blue* by Janice Lee (Civil Coping Mechanisms, 2016).

If only you didn't have to shove your living in my face: the title uses a phrase from (and is inspired by) the poem 'the horse could die' by Emma Jeremy, from *Sad Thing Angry* (Out-Spoken Press, 2023).

Essay on Craft: inspired by Ocean Vuong's 'Essay on Craft' (*Poetry*, July/Augst 2017).

His absence is like the sky, spread over everything: most of the title is a line from C.S. Lewis *A Grief Observed* (Faber and Faber, 2015). The original line is 'Her absence is like the sky, spread over everything.'

without: quote from 'Name' by Rachel Eliza Griffiths, from *Seeing the Body* (W. W. Norton & Company, 2020).

Acknowledgements

A huge thank you to Arts Council England for a DYCP grant that enabled me to revisit my mother's burial place, gave precious time for research and writing, and allowed me to attend two Arvon at Home courses.

Thanks also to The Society of Authors for an Authors' Foundation Grant for a work in progress.

I am eternally grateful to the editors of all the wonderful real world and online journals/anthologies in which earlier versions of some of these poems appeared:

Atrium, Black Nore Review, Butcher's Dog, Fenland Poetry Journal, Finished Creatures, Gutter Magazine, Hog River Press, Ink Sweat and Tears, London Grip, Obsessed With Pipework, ONE ART, Poetry Wales, Poetry Worth Hearing, Strix, Under the Radar, Whirlagust IV

A huge thanks to the inspirational Jane Commane and the Nine Arches team – I feel extremely lucky to have such an attentive editor.

Big thanks also to the tutors on the Arvon at home and other workshops I attended with my DYCP grant for giving me new ways into my subject matter, and for invaluable tutorial feedback (especially Tara Bergin, Yomi Sode, Rebecca Goss, Victoria Kennefick). The title sequence 'Grey Time' was written as a result of a prose poem workshop with Carrie Etter.

A heartfelt thank you to Jinny Fisher for offering me use of her studio for a writing retreat and to Rachael Clyne for taxiing me to where my mum is buried.

Massive gratitude to the poetry friends/workshopping groups who have put many of these poems through their paces: Heidi Williamson, Hannah Linden, Rachael Clyne, Jinny Fisher, Michelle Diaz, Jess Mookherjee, Moniza Alvi, Laura Scott, Alison Winch, Kathryn Symonds, Elizabeth Lewis Williams and all the members (past and present) of Norwich Stanza. I would especially like to thank Heidi for her close reading of the MS at a critical stage!

Lastly a big thanks to all the poets whose work has inspired and informed my own and for the lovely readers who read my work.

And last (but never least) to my son Natty Peterkin for the amazing artwork and everything else.